• Bart

MW00895800

YORK
Streetfinder
COLOUR ATLAS

Contents

Bartholomew
A Division of HarperCollins*Publishers*

KEY TO MAP PAGES

Printed in Hong Kong

ISBN 0 7028 2166 7
F/B 6493 CDNU

This street atlas of the city of York has been compiled and drawn from aerial photography.

Legend
Légende, Zeichenerklärung

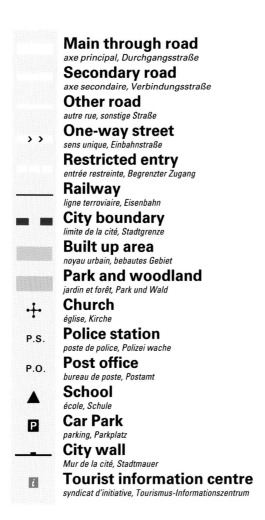

Main through road
axe principal, Durchgangsstraße

Secondary road
axe secondaire, Verbindungsstraße

Other road
autre rue, sonstige Straße

One-way street
sens unique, Einbahnstraße

Restricted entry
entrée restreinte, Begrenzter Zugang

Railway
ligne terroviaire, Eisenbahn

City boundary
limite de la cité, Stadtgrenze

Built up area
noyau urbain, bebautes Gebiet

Park and woodland
jardin et forêt, Park und Wald

Church
église, Kirche

Police station
poste de police, Polizei wache

Post office
bureau de poste, Postamt

School
école, Schule

Car Park
parking, Parkplatz

City wall
Mur de la cité, Stadtmauer

Tourist information centre
syndicat d'initiative, Tourismus-Informationszentrum

SCALE

Scale of main map pages, **1:11,000**

0   ¼   ½   ¾ mile

0   0.5   1.0 kilometre

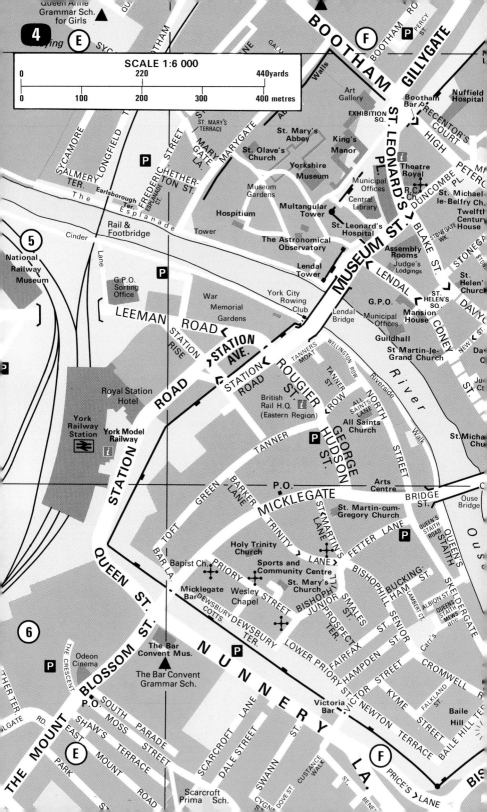

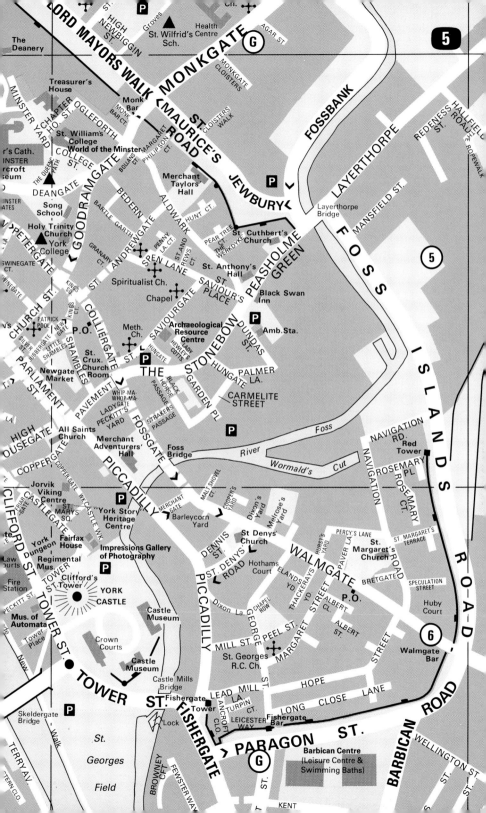

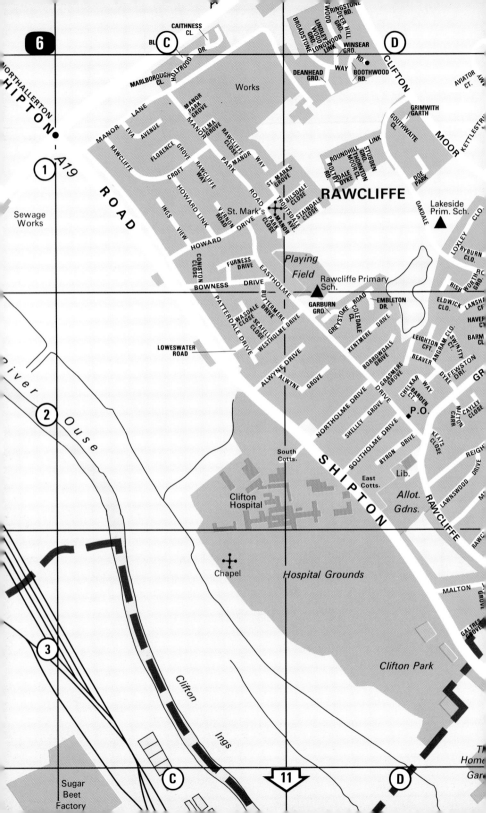

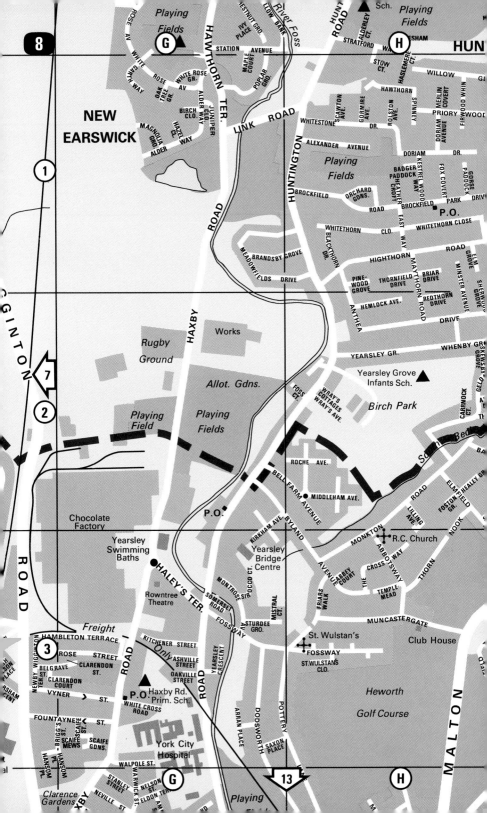

Asda
Superstore

JOCKEY LANE

Pigeoncote
Industrial
Park

Water Sports
Centre

KATHRYN AVE.
JULIA AVE.
JOCKEY AVE.

LANE

ROAD MALTON A

Amenity
Lake

1

Thornfield
Farm

MALTON

Ryethorpe
Grange Farm

2

Rugby
Football
Ground

ROAD

Playing

Fields

ELMPARK VIEW
ELMPARK WAY
ELMPARK VALE
GR. WOODLANDS
ELMLANDS GROVE
GROVE
WESTLANDS
MEADOW WAY

GREEN SWARD
GREENFIELD
GREEN PARK
GREEN MEADOWS
LAWNWAY
DRIVE

Christ Ch.

PASTURE LANE

RYECROFT CLOSE
BEANS WAY
BECKWITH CLO.
HILL VIEW

GALTRES
GALTRES AVENUE
LARCHFIELD
ROAD

3

LANE

ALGARTH RD.
SANDSTOCK ROAD
ALGARTH RISE
HIGH OAKS
THE GLADE
ASHLEY PARK
CEDAR GROVE
SPRINGFIELD WAY
SPRINGFIELD CLOSE

P.O.

WHITBY
CAEDMON CLOSE
WHITBY DRIVE
ASH CLOSE
APPLECROFT RD.
HAZEL GARTH
ASHLEY PARK CRESCENT

TOCKTON
OAKLAND AVE.
OAKLAND DRIVE
HERBERTS WAY
HEMPLAND
HEMPLAND DRIVE

J 14 K

Allot.
Hempland
Prim. Sch.

Apple Tr
Farm

Map Labels

Grid references: 10 4 5 6

Top row: A — ROAD A59 — B

Roads and Streets

WESTVIEW CLOSE
TRENCHARD ROAD
PORTAL ROAD
POPPLETON LANE
Manor C. of E. Sec. Sch.
Playing Field
LANGHOLME DRIVE
FARFIELD
MILL GATES
THE PADDOCK
PADDOCK WAY
PLANTATION DRIVE
PLANT GRO
P.O.
BOROUGH

NEWLANDS DRIVE
SHERWOOD GROVE
ALBION AVENUE
NORMAN DRIVE
GROVE
LIDGETT GROVE
WHEATLANDS
GROVE
SHIRLEY AVENUE
CRANBROOK
Methodist Ch.
Lidgett Gro. Sch.
OUSEBURN
AVENUE
SITWELL GROVE
CRANBROOK
MELWOOD GROVE
GRAYSHON DRIVE
MELWOOD GROVE
ALMSFORD DRIVE
ALMSFORD
CELTIC CLOSE
ROAD

Northfield Sch.
Playing Field
P.O.
Carr Infants Sch.
Playing Fields
Carr Junior Sch.
JORVIK CLO.
GREENSBOROUGH AV.
PRESTWICK CT.
OSTMAN ROAD
SMEATON GROVE
Allot. Gdns.
VYN CLOSE
WOODLEA GROVE

Knapton

BACK LANE
VILLAGE STREET
D R I.
MUIRFIELD WAY
JUTE ROAD
KENRICK PLACE
TOSTIG
FAWKES DRIVE
DANEBURY DRIVE
WOODLEA
WOOD CRE
LOCHRIN PL.
TURNBERRY
BIRKDALE GRO.
CARNOUSTIE CLO.
AVENUE
VIKING ROAD
DANE
AVENUE
DANEBURY CT.
WOODLEA
WOODLEA A

WFIELD LANE
TEN THORN LANE
LANE
KNAPTON LANE
MELANDER CLO.
COURCEY GROVE
MOWBRAY DRIVE
ROAD
DANEBURY CRES.
DRIVE

BECKFIELD
JUTE
RAVEN GRO.
GRESLEY CT.
BECKFIELD PL.
STAITHES CLOSE
BEECH AVENUE

BLAND
BRIAR AVE.
COLLINGHAM PL.
FELLBROOK AVENUE
RUNSWICK AVE.
DANEBURY DRIVE
ROSEDALE
GRANGER PL.
CHESTNUT GR.
GROVE
ACOM

B1224
WETHERBY
ROAD
THE GREEN
YORK
KIRK
VIEW
CHURCH MS
St. Stephen's
OAK RISE
CROSS

Chapel
CHAPEL FIELDS
BRIDLE WAY
FIELDS
RIDGEWAY
CROFT SIDE
CROFT WAY
Acomb Green
THE GREEN
STREET
GROVE TER.
BRAMHAM GROVE
BARKSTON PLACE
ROAD
MARSTON CR.
MARSTON AVENUE
ACOMB MS.
SOUTH VIEW
CHAPEL TER.
Liby.
P

Fields
BRAMHAM
ROAD
AVENUE
St. Aidan's
RYLATT PLACE
Baptist Ch.
Rec. Grd.
RIDGEWAY
ALEXA CT.
CHANCERY
FRONT
Methodist Ch.
GALE FARM CT.
LOWFIELDS DRIVE
AVENUE

HESSAY PLACE
BARKSTON GROVE
BRAMHAM
HAMMERTON CLOSE
WALTON PLACE
LANE
VESPER DRIVE
GALE
DIJON
KIR CRESCENT
Lowfield Sch.
Playing Fi

CHAPEL FIELDS
THE WRANGLE RD.
HOTHAM AVENUE
PARKER
LANE
BACHELOR HILL
HADDON CLO.
VESPER DRI.
Low Fiel

A — 16 — B

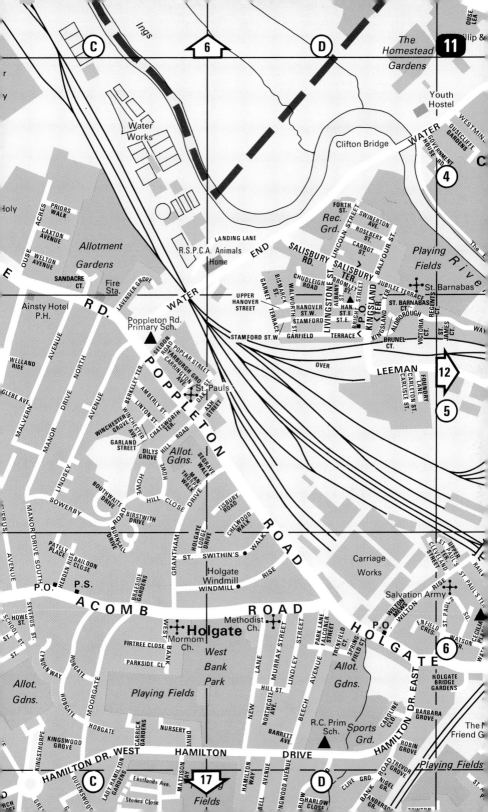

Ings

C

6

D

The Homestead Gardens

Youth Hostel

Water Works

Clifton Bridge

WATER

OUSECLIFFE GARDENS

GOVERNMENT HOUSE RD.

WESTMIN...

OUSE LEA...

illip &

C

4

LANDING LANE

R.S.P.C.A. Animals Home

END

Rec. Grd.

FORTH ST.

SWINERTON AVE.

ROSEBERY ST.

LINCOLN STREET

CARNOT ST.

BALFOUR ST.

Playing Fields

River

The...

St. Barnabas

Holy

Allotment Gardens

ACRES

PRIORS WALK

CAXTON AVENUE

WELTON AVENUE

OUSE

SANDACRE CT.

Fire Sta.

LAVENDER GROVE

Ainsty Hotel P.H.

E

RD.

WATER

SALISBURY RD.

SALISBURY TER.

SALISBURY TER.

CHUDLEIGH ROAD

BISMARCK ST.

WALWORTH ST.

GARNET TERRACE

HANOVER ST.W.

STAMFORD

ALBANY ST.

BROMLEY ST.

BRIGHT STREET

HAN. ST.E.

JUBILEE TERRACE

KINGSLAND TER.

KINGSLAND TER.

ST. BARNABAS CT.

ALDBOROUGH

REGENTS

VICTORIA CT.

ST. JAMES CT.

ST. BARNABAS CT.

WA...

UPPER HANOVER STREET

STAMFORD ST.W.

HANOVER ST.W.

STAMFORD

GARFIELD

TERRACE

P.O.

BRUNEL CT.

OVER

LEEMAN

FOUNDRY LANE

CARLETON ST.

CARLISLE ST.

12

5

Poppleton Rd. Primary Sch.

SELDON ROAD

POPLAR STREET

HAMBURGH GRO.

CARRINGTON AVE.

OAK ST.

St. Pauls

BERKELEY TER.

AMBERLY ST.

LINTON ST.

CHATSWORTH TER.

ASH STREET

HILL ROAD

WELLAND RISE

MALVERN

MANOR DRIVE

AVENUE NORTH

AVENUE

WINCHESTER GROVE

WINCHESTER AVE.

GARLAND STREET

DILYS GROVE

HOWE

Allot. Gdns.

SEGRAVE WALK

MAN. THORN WALK

GLEBE AVE.

LINDSEY

SOWERBY

BOUTHWAITE DRIVE

ROAD BIRSTWITH DRIVE

BURSALL DRIVE

BAILDON CLOSE

HILL CLOSE DRIVE

TISBURY ROAD

CHELWOOD WALK

WALK

ROAD

Carriage Works

MANOR DRIVE SOUTH

AVENUE

PATELY PLACE

HEBDEN RISE

BRAESIDE GARDENS

GRANTHAM ST.

HOLGATE LODGE DRIVE

ST. SWITHIN'S

Holgate Windmill

WINDMILL

RISE

Salvation Army

RISE

ST. PAULS

UPPER CLEVELAND STREET

ST. PAUL'S TER.

ST. PAUL'S SQ.

WILTON MEWS

WILTON

RAIL...

ST. PAUL'S STR...

P.O.

CECILIA...

6

WATSON ST.

SEVERUS ST.

HOWE ST.

SCHOOL ST.

LYNDEN WAY

P.O.

P.S.

ACOMB

ROAD

HOLGATE

ENFIELD CRES.

BARBARA GROVE

HOLGATE BRIDGE GARDENS

Holgate

Mormom Ch.

Methodist Ch.

WEST BANK

West Bank Park

FIRTREE CLOSE

PARKSIDE CL.

NEW LANE

MURRAY STREET

HILL ST.

NORTHCOTE AVE.

LINDLEY STREET

BEECH AVENUE

PARK LANE

FALCONER STREET

TRENFIELD STREET

SPRINGFIELD CT.

Allot. Gdns.

CAROLINE CLO.

ROBIN GROVE

NIGEL GR.

Allot. Gdns.

HOBGATE

MOORGATE

HOBGATE

KINGSWOOD GROVE

CARRICK GARDENS

NURSERY DRIVE

R.C. Prim Sch.

Sports Grd.

BARRETT AVE.

BANDERSON GR.

TREVOR GROVE

The... Friend G...

Playing Fields

KINGSTHORPE

C

HAMILTON DR. WEST

LADY HAMILTON GARDENS

Eastlands Ave.

Stones Close

17

Fields

HAMILTON

MATTISON...

HAMILTON WAY

BELL LANE

AVENUE

RINGWOOD AVENUE

HARLOW CLOSE...

DRIVE

CLIVE GRO.

BANK...

D

HAMILTON DR. EAST

ROAD

Playing Fields

QUEENSWOOD...

TOWTON...

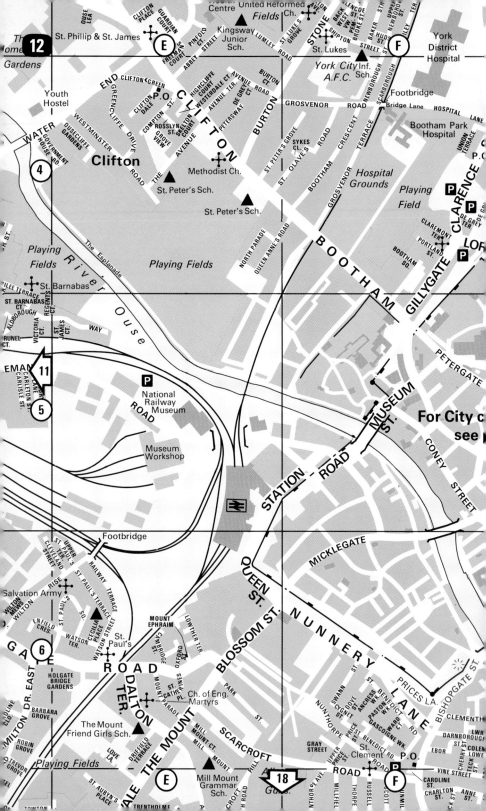

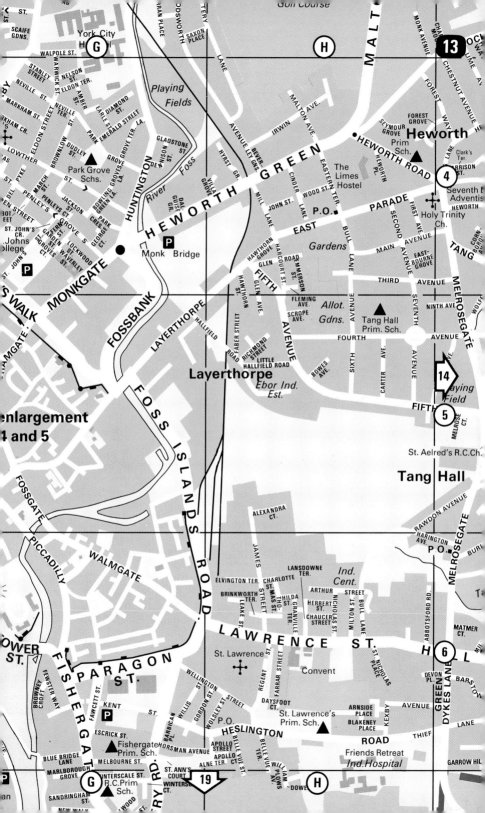

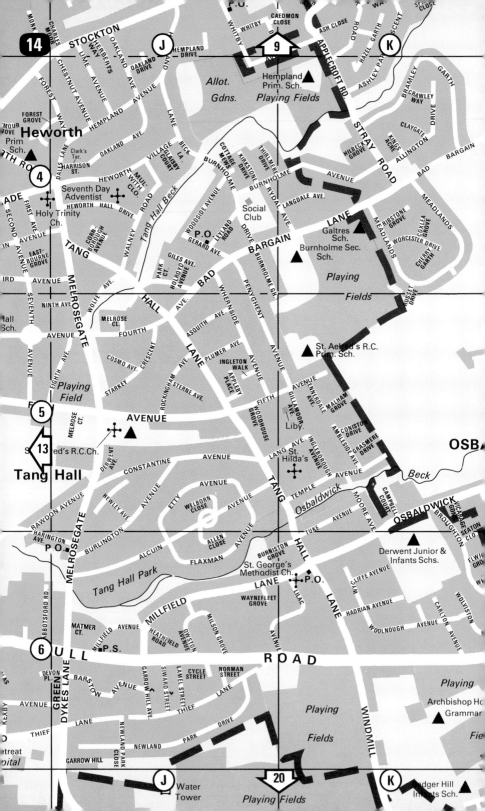

ple Tree
Farm

4

MU

YOR

5

Y O

MURTON

OUTGANG LA.

YEW TREE MS.

GALIGAP LA.

DWICK   VILLAGE

CK

T FIELD

LANE

St.
Thomas's Ch.

Liby.

OSBALDWICK

Playing

ST. THOMAS'S CLOSE

THIRLBEEY WAY

CHURCH   ROAD

KIRKDALE ROAD

BROOKLANDS

AVIS GROVE

TRANBY

WENSLEYDALE DR.

WYDALE

Field

ST. MARY'S GRO.

FARNDALE AVE.

HIGH FIELD

BEDALE AVENUE

ROAD

LINK

T EYES

THE   LEYES

P.O.

HAZELWOOD

AVENUE

GIVERDALE GROVE

THIRKLEBY

SHALLOW DALE GROVE

ESKDALE

PINELANDS

BRACKEN HILL

LYNDALE AVE.

BAYSDALE AVE.

CANHAM GROVE

BRANSDALE CR.

HEATHER BANK

WAY

CAVENDISH GROVE

Depot

RD.

R O A D

6

H U L L

YARBURGH

HESKETH BANK

LOW MILL CLO.

LANE

VANBRUGH DRIVE

KIMBERLOWS WOODS HILL

PINE WOOD HILL

DRIVE

HOLBURN PADDOCK

FERNWAY

DERAMORE

RAMORE WEST

*Playing
Fields*

BAD

WOOD CR.

CRESCENT

**Badger
Hill**

FIELD

LANE

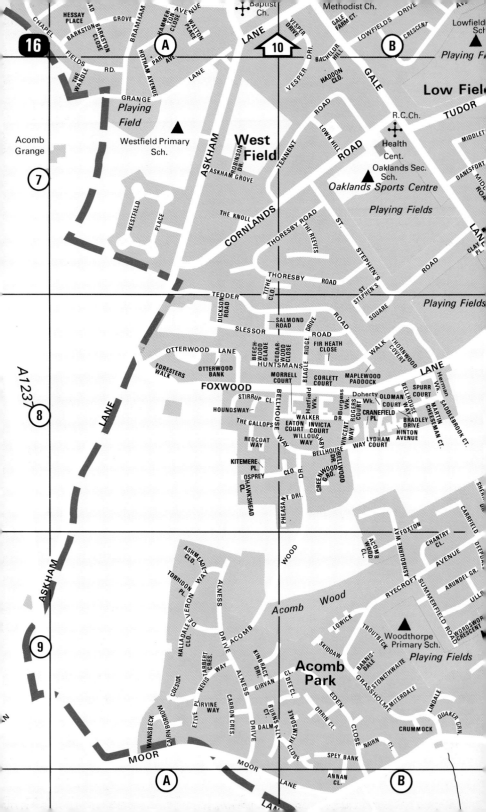

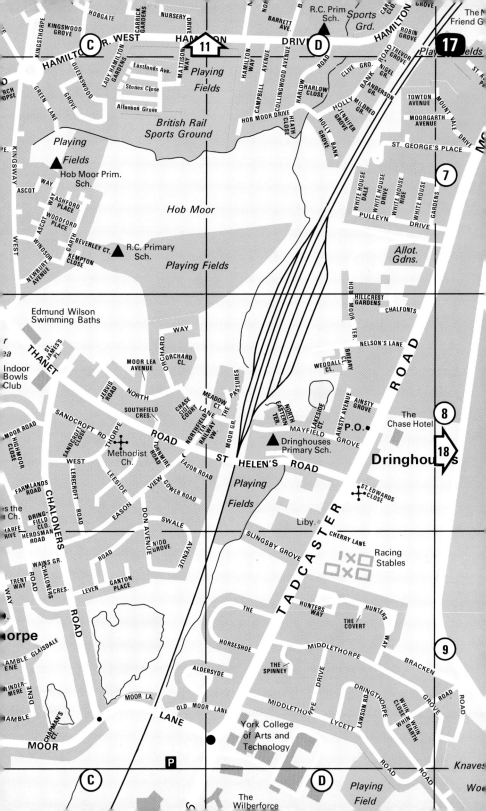

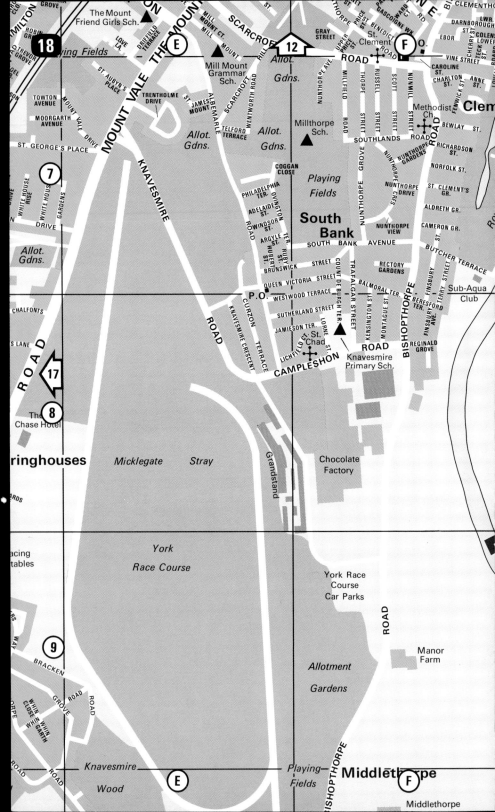

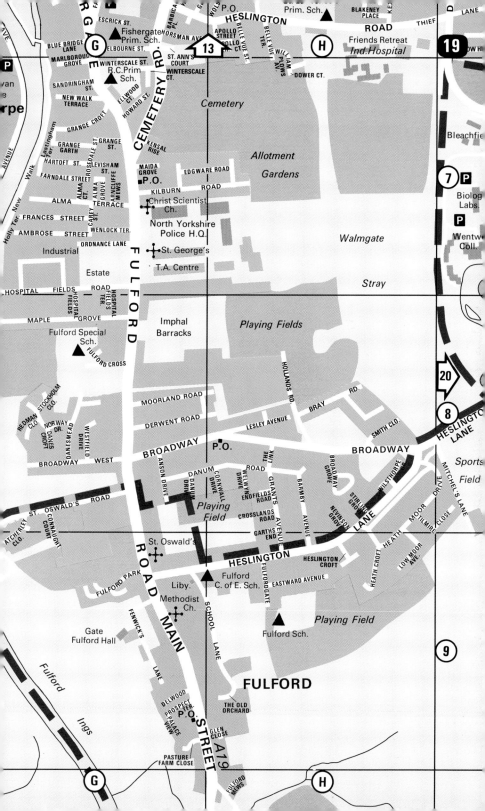

LANE

GARROW HILL

NEWLAND PARK CLOSE

NEWLAND

PARK DRIVE

J

14

Fields

WINDMILL

K

Field

Water Tower

Playing Fields

Badger Hill Infants Sch.

UNIVERSITY

P

Library

Bleachfield

I.R.I.S.S.

P

Computer Sc. Bldgs.

Alcuin Coll.

Chemistry Labs.

Science Park

7

Music & Concert Hall

P

Vanbrugh Coll.

ROAD

LANE

UNIVERSITY

P

Biology Labs.

Central Hall

Language Centre

Langwith Coll.

OF YORK

Heslington Ch.

P

(York Film Thea.)

Derwent Coll.

Playing Field

Wentworth Coll.

Goodricke Coll.

Vice-Chancellor's House

Heslington Hall

SCHOOL

HESLINGTO

P

P

Physics Labs.

MAIN

STREET

HESLINGTON CT.

LANE

19

James College

Maintenance Bldgs.

WALNUT CL.

MAIN

HALL PARK

P

P.O.

LLOYD CLOSE

8

Edens Court

STREET

LOW

HESLINGTON

LANE

St. Lawrence Court

COMMON

Sports Field

MITCHEL'S LANE

MOOR DRIVE

TILMIRE CLOSE

WAY

THORPE GR.

HEATH

LOW MOOR AVE.

9

Places of interest in York

York - A Short History

York, for centuries the northern capital of England, owes its origins to the River Ouse which flows through the old town centre and to the Romans who built the fortress town and named it Eboracum. After their withdrawal in the fifth century it was the Anglo Saxon invaders who took control of the city and built the first cathedral, but these too were ousted when the Vikings captured York and named it Jorvik.

After William the Conqueror defeated Harold at the Battle of Hastings, England was ruled by the Normans and under them York flourished, particularly as a port and a centre for the wool trade. At this time the present city walls and gates were built.

York suffered a decline in the sixteenth century with the dwindling of the wool trade and Henry VIII's dissolution of the monasteries, but it enjoyed a renaissance in the eighteenth century when handsome Georgian houses and buildings began to replace the decayed medieval ones. In the nineteenth and twentieth centuries the city again grew to be as important as ever it had been, becoming a great railway centre and ecclesiastical headquarters.

Archaeological Research Centre (The ARC), St. Saviourgate G5 5

Situated in the beautifully restored medieval church of St. Saviour, the ARC offers the opportunity to have hands-on experience of archaeology. Visitors are encouraged to sort and date authentic finds, try ancient crafts such as spinning and weaving and even plan an excavation using computer technology.

Assembly Rooms, Blake Street F5 4

Designed by Lord Burlington and paid for by public subscription, these elegant eighteenth century rooms were the centre of fashionable Georgian society functions, especially in the central hall distinguished by its 48 supporting Corinthian columns.

The Bar Convent Museum, Blossom Street E6 4

A pilgrimage through 300 years of Christian history in York and in the life of England's oldest, active post-reformation convent which has a magnificent domed chapel.

Castle Museum, Tower Street G6 5

A remarkable record of everyday life through the centuries, including the Kirkgate—an authentic reconstruction of a Victorian street complete with shops and houses.

City Art Gallery, Exhibition Square F5 4

Especially noted for its Italian collection the Gallery has works by the York—born artist William Etty and is known for its Lycett Green collection of Old Masters.

Clifford's Tower, Tower Street G6 5

The original wooden castle, built by William the Conqueror, was destroyed by fire in 1190 and the existing stone castle Keep was built in the thirteenth century.

Fairfax House, Castlegate G6 5

Described as a classic architectural masterpiece of its age, this is the finest Georgian town house in York and is furnished with elegant period pieces from the Noel Terry collection of furnture and clocks.

Friargate Museum Lower Friargate F6 5

A collection of more than 50 wax models of famous people including such tableaux as the 'Dukes of York' and the 'Royal Family'.

Guildhall, Coney Street F5 4

Badly damaged during an air raid in 1942 the Guildhall is a restoration of the original fifteenth century Commonhall, although the Inner Chamber escaped serious damage in 1942 and is worth visiting.

Jorvik Viking Centre, Coppergate F5 4

This exact reconstruction of a Viking street is built on the site of the original archaelogical excavation and visitors are taken through it in 'time cars' from which they experience the authentic sights, sounds and smells of Jorvik — Viking York.

Kings Manor, Exhibition Square F5 4

Originally the home of the Abbot of St. Mary's Abbey, it became the official residence of the King's Council of the North after the dissolution of the monasteries and is now part of the University of York.

The Mansion House, St. Helen's Square F5 4

Built in the eighteennth century this is the official residence of the Lord Mayor of York, during his term of office and also contains the civic plate.

Merchant Adventurers' Hall, Fossgate G5 5

This magnificent, timbered, medieval Guild Hall, which was built in the fourteenth century, is one of the best surviving examples and is noted for its fine timbered roof in the Great Hall.

Merchant Taylors' Hall, Aldwark G5 5

Built in the fourteenth century this timber-roofed hall has been used by the Company of Merchant Taylors since the fifteenth century and although it was disused for many years has been completely restored by the Guild.

Museum of Automata, Tower Street F6 5

This museum houses a collection of ingenious machines spanning 2000 years which illustrates the story of automata from simple articulated figurines from ancient civilisations to modern robots.

National Railway Museum, Leeman Road E5 4

Part of London's Science Museum, the Railway museum has one of the finest collections of British railway engineering heritage in Britain, if not the world and in the Great Hall an historic collection of locomotives and rolling stock (including Queen Victoria's Saloon) are arranged around two original turntables.

St. Anthony's Hall, Peasholme Green G5 5

This medieval Guildhall, built in the fifteenth century, is now the Borthwick Institute of Historical Research, part of the University of York.

St. Mary's Abbey, Museum Gardens F5 4

Originally founded in 1080 as a Benedictine Abbey, the existing ruins date from the medieval period and form part of the setting for the medieval 'Mystery Plays' which are re-enacted in the Museum Gardens.

St. William's College, College Street G5 5

This timbered, fifteenth century building was originally a college for Minster Chantry priests until its dissolution by Henry VIII a century later. During the Civil War Charles I had his printing press and Royal Mint housed here.

Treasurer's House (NT) Minster Yard G5 5

Set on the site of old Roman barracks, the original house was the home of the Treasurers of York Minster, but only part of this remains and the present house, which dates from the seventeenth and eighteenth centuries, has a collection of pictures and furniture from many periods.

Twelth Century House, Stonegate F5 4

These fragmentary remains of a Norman house have been restored and are the oldest existing in York.

Yorkshire Museum, Museum Gardens F5 4

Situated in the botanic gardens, where there is also an astronomical observatory, the museum houses impressive collections of archaeology, natural history, geology and pottery, including excellent displays of Roman and medieval treasures.

Yorkshire Museum of Farming, Murton (2 miles east of York)

This museum traces the history of farming developments and has demonstrations of country crafts.

York Story Heritage Centre, Castlegate G6 5

The history and architecture of the city explored through the use of models, reconstructions and audio-visual presentation.

City Walls and Bars

Extending for three miles around the city, the walls and gateways built in the thirteenth century by the Normans have withstood the efforts of City Councils to demolish them for building purposes and now provide a fascinating walk affording fine views over the city.

York Minster F5 5

The triple towers of the great Minster dominate York. The fifth church to stand upon the site, it is built on cruciform style and its chief characteristics, inside as outside, are great beauty and impressive size and space. The magnificent stained glass in the Minster - much of it medieval - is of tremendous interest. In the south transept the great Rose window displays a design entwining the red and white roses of Lancaster and York respectively, and commemorates the wedding in 1486 of Henry VII to Elizabeth of York, which at last united the two warring 'Roses'. The Choir, the north transept, and the octagonal Chapter House are very fine, the roof vaulting being among the best examples to be seen anywhere. Beyond the Close to the north of the Minster are the Deanery and the Library (Early English), the latter the repository of many literary treasures. The Minster itself is rich in historic possessions and is the seat of the second See of England, its Archbishop being next in rank and precedence to the Primate of All England, the Archbishop of Canterbury.

A fire in 1984 badly damaged the roof of the south transept but brave firefighting prevented it spreading to the rest of the Cathedral.

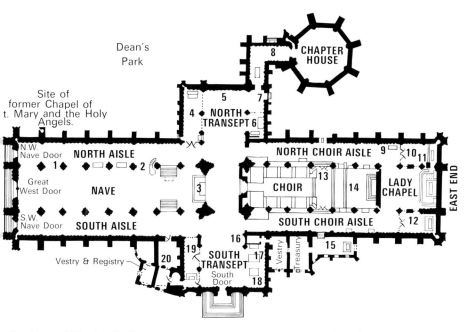

1	Altar of The Lord's Prayer	11	Tomb of Archbishop Scrope
2	Nave Pulpit	12	All Saints' Chapel
3	Nave Altar	13	Entrance to Crypt
4	St. John's Chapel	14	High Altar
5	Five Sisters Window	15	Zouche Chapel
6	St. Nicholas' Chapel	16	Archbishop Thomson Monument
7	Astronomical Clock	17	Tomb of Archbishop Walter de Grey
8	Vestibule	18	Dean Duncombe Monument
9	Effigy of Prince William of Hatfield	19	St. George's Chapel
10	St. Stephen's Chapel	20	Bookshop

INDEX TO STREETS

General Abbreviations

App.	Approach	Gdns.	Gardens	Ri.	Rise
Av.	Avenue	Grn.	Green	Rd.	Road
Bdy.	Broadway	Gro.	Grove	S.	South
Bldgs.	Buildings	Ho.	House	St.	Street
Cft.	Croft	La.	Lane	Ter.	Terrace
Clo.	Close	Ms.	Mews	Vills.	Villas
Cotts.	Cottages	Mt.	Mount	Vw.	View
Cres.	Crescent	N.	North	W.	West
Ct.	Court	Par.	Parade	Wk.	Walk
Dr.	Drive	Pk.	Park	Yd.	Yard
E.	East	Pl.	Place		
Est.	Estate	Prom.	Promenade		

Name	No.	Grid	Name	No.	Grid	Name	No.	Grid
Bedale Av.	15	L5	Branton Pl.	10	A6	Carnoustie Clo.	10	A5
Bede Av.	7	F3	Bray Rd.	19	H8	Caroline Clo.	11	D6
Bedern	5	G5	Breary Clo.	17	D8	Caroline St.	18	F7
Beech Av.	11	D6	Bretgate	5	G6	Carr La.	10	B5
Beech Glade	8	H1	Briar Av.	10	A6	Carrfield	16	B8
Beech Gro.	10	B5	Briar Dr.	8	H1	Carrick Gdns.	11	C6
Beechwood Glade	16	A8	Bridge La.	12	F4	Carrington Av.	11	C5
Belgrave St.	7	F3	Bridge St.	4	F6	Carrnock Ct.	7	H2
Bell Fm. Av.	8	G2	Bridle Way	10	A6	Carron Cres.	16	A9
Belle Vue St.	13	H6	Briggs St.	8	G3	Carrs La.	4	F6
Belle Vue Ter.	13	H6	Bright St.	11	D5	Carter Av.	13	H5
Bellhouse Way	16	B8	Brinkworth Ter.	13	H6	Castle Mills Bri.	5	G6
Bellwood Dr.	16	B8	Broad St.	18	F7	Castle Wk.	5	G6
Belmont Clo.	6	D2	Broadstone Way	6	D1	Castlegate	5	F6
Beresford Ter.	18	F8	Broadway	19	G8	Cavendish Gro.	15	L6
Berkeley Ter.	11	C5	Broadway Gro.	19	H8	Caxton Av.	11	C4
Beverley Ct.	17	C7	Broadway W.	19	G8	Cayley Clo.	6	D2
Beverley Gdns.	13	H4	Brockfield Pk. Dr.	8	H1	Cecilia Pl.	12	E6
Bewlay St.	18	F7	Brockfield Rd.	8	H1	Cedar Gro.	9	K3
Bilsdale Clo.	6	D1	Bromley St.	11	D4	Cedarwood Clo.	16	A8
Birch Clo.	8	G1	Brompton Rd.	7	E3	Celtic Clo.	10	B4
Birch Copse	17	C7	Brook St.	12	F4	Cemetery Rd.	19	G7
Birkdale Gro.	10	A5	Brooklands	15	L5	Chalfonts	17	D8
Birstwith Dr.	11	C5	Broughton Way	14	K5	Chaloners Cres.	17	C9
Bishopgate St.	4	F6	Browney Cft.	13	G6	Chaloners Rd.	17	C8
Bishophill Junior	4	F6	Brownlow St.	13	G4	Chancery Ct.	10	B6
Bishophill Senior	4	F6	Brunel Ct.	11	D5	Chantry Clo.	16	B9
Bishops Way	14	K6	Brunswick St.	18	E7	Chapel Flds. Rd.	10	A6
Bismarck St.	11	D4	Buckingham St.	4	F6	Chapel Row	5	G6
Black Horse Pas.	5	G5	Bull La.	13	H6	Chapel Ter.	10	B6
Blackthorne Dr.	8	H1	Bull La., Heworth	13	H4	Chapman's Ct.	17	C9
Blake St.	4	F5	Bur Dike Av.	7	E3	Chapter Ho. St.	4	F5
Blakeley Gro.	6	D1	Burgess Wk.	16	B8	Charles Moor	9	J3
Blakeney Pl.	13	H6	Burlington Av.	14	J6	Charlotte St.	13	H6
Bland La.	10	A6	Burnholme Av.	14	J4	Charlton St.	18	F7
Blenheim Ct.	6	C1	Burnholme Dr.	14	J4	Chaseside Ct.	17	C8
Blossom St.	4	E6	Burnholme Gro.	14	J4	Chatsworth Ter.	11	C5
Blue Bri. La.	13	G6	Burniston Gro.	14	J6	Chaucer St.	13	H6
Bollans Ct.	5	G5	Burns Ct.	16	A9	Chelkar Way	6	D2
Boltby Rd.	6	D1	Burnsall Dr.	11	C6	Chelwood Wk.	11	D5
Bootham	4	F4	Burrill Av.	7	F3	Cherry Garth	14	K4
Bootham Bar	4	F5	Burton Av.	7	F3	Cherry La.	17	D9
Bootham Cres.	12	F4	Burton Ct.	12	E4	Cherry St.	12	F6
Bootham Row	4	F4	Burton Stone La.	12	E4	Chestnut Av.	14	J4
Bootham Sq.	12	F4	Butcher Ter.	18	F7	Chestnut Gro.	10	B6
Bootham Ter.	4	E4	Buttermere Dr.	6	C2	Chestnut Gro.	8	G1
Boothwood Rd.	6	D1	Byland Av.	8	H2	Cheviot Clo.	8	H1
Boroughbridge Rd.	10	B4	Byron Dr.	6	D2	Chudleigh Rd.	11	D4
Borrowdale Dr.	6	D2				Church La.,	4	F5
Bouthwaite Dr.	11	C5	Caedmon Clo.	9	J3	Bishopthorpe		
Bowes Av.	13	H5	Cairnborrow	16	A9	Church Ms.	10	B6
Bowland Way	7	E2	Caithness Clo.	6	C1	Church Rd.	15	L5
Bowling Grn. La.	13	G4	Caldbeck Clo.	7	E2	Church St.	4	F5
Bowness Dr.	6	C1	Cambridge St.	12	E6	Cinder La.	4	E5
Bracken Hill	15	L6	Cameron Gro.	18	F7	Cinder La., Heworth	13	H4
Bracken Rd.	17	D9	Campbell Av.	17	D7	Claremont Ter.	12	F4
Bradley Dr.	16	B8	Campbell Ct.	14	K5	Clarence St.	12	F4
Braeside Gdns.	11	C6	Campleshon Rd.	18	E8	Clarendon Ct.	8	G3
Bramble Dene	17	C9	Canham Gro.	15	L6	Clarendon St.	8	G3
Bramham Av.	10	A6	Carey St.	19	G7	Clarks Ter.	14	J4
Bramham Gro.	10	A6	Carl St.	18	F7	Clay Pl.	16	B7
Bramham Rd.	10	A6	Carleton St.	11	D5	Claygate	14	K4
Bramley Garth	14	K4	Carlisle St.	11	D5	Clement St.	12	F6
Brandsby Gro.	8	G1	Carlton Av.	14	K6	Clementhorpe	12	F6
Bransdale Cres.	15	L6	Carmelite St.	5	G5	Cleveland St.	11	D6
Bransholme Dr.	7	E1	Carnot St.	11	D4	Cleveland Way	8	H1

Fetter La.	4	F6	Garfield Ter.	11	D5	Greensborough	10	A5	
Feversham Cres.	7	F3	Garland St.	11	C5	Av.			
Fewster Way	13	G6	Garlands, The	7	E2	Greenwood Gro.	16	B8	
Fewston Dr.	6	D2	Garnet Ter.	11	D4	Gresley Ct.	10	B5	
Field La.,	20	K7	Garrow Hill	14	J6	Greystoke Rd.	6	D2	
Heslington			Garrow Hill Av.	14	J6	Grimwith Garth	6	D1	
Field Vw.	7	F3	Garth Ter.	7	F3	Grosvenor Rd.	12	F4	
Fifth Av.	13	H4	Garth Way	8	G1	Grosvenor Ter.	12	F4	
Filey Ter.	7	F3	Garths End	19	H9	Grove Ter.	10	B6	
Finkle St.	4	F5	Gascoigne Wk.	12	F6	Grove Ter. La.	13	G4	
Finsbury Av.	18	F8	Geldof Rd.	8	H2	Grove Vw.	12	E4	
Finsbury St.	18	F7	George Cayley Dr.	7	E1	Groves Ct.	13	G4	
Fir Heath Clo.	16	B8	George Ct.	13	G4	Groves La.	13	G4	
First Av.	13	H4	George Hudson St.	4	F5	Guardian Ct.	7	E3	
Firtree Clo.	11	C6	George St.	5	G6				
Firwood Whin	8	H1	Gerard Av.	14	J4	Haddon Clo.	16	B7	
Fishergate	13	G6	Giles Av.	14	J4	Hadrian Av.	14	K6	
Fishergate Bar	5	G6	Gillamoor Av.	14	K5	Haleys Ter.	8	G3	
Fitzroy Ter.	5	G6	Gillygate	4	F5	Halifax Ct.	7	E2	
Flavian Gro.	6	D3	Girvan Clo.	16	A9	Hall Pk.	20	K7	
Flaxman Av.	14	J6	Givendale Gro.	15	L6	Halladale Clo.	16	A9	
Fleming Av.	13	H5	Glade, The	9	K3	Hallfield Rd.	13	G5	
Florence Gro.	6	C1	Gladstone St.	13	G4	Hambleton Av.	14	K5	
Forest Gro.	13	H4	Gladstone St.,	10	B6	Hambleton Ter.	7	F3	
Forest Way	13	H4	Acomb			Hambleton Way	8	H1	
Foresters Wk.	16	A8	Glaisby Ct.	14	J4	Hamilton Dr.	11	C6	
Forth St.	11	D4	Glaisdale	17	C9	Hamilton Dr. E.	11	D6	
Foss Bri.	5	G5	Glebe Av.	11	C5	Hamilton Dr. W.	17	C7	
Foss Ct.	7	H2	Glen Av.	13	H4	Hamilton Way	17	D7	
Foss Islands Rd.	5	G5	Glen Clo.	19	H9	Hammerton Clo.	10	A6	
Fossbank	5	G5	Glen Rd.	13	H4	Hampden St.	4	F6	
Fossgate	5	G5	Glencoe St.	7	F3	Hanover St. E.	11	D5	
Fossway	8	G3	Glenridding	16	B9	Hanover St. W.	11	D5	
Foston Gro.	8	H2	Goodramgate	5	G5	Hansom Pl.	8	G3	
Foundry La.	11	D5	Gordon St.	13	G6	Harcourt St.	13	H4	
Fountayne St.	7	F3	Gormire Av.	8	H1	Harington Av.	13	H6	
Fourth Av.	13	H5	Gorse Paddock	8	H1	Harlow Clo.	17	D7	
Fox Covert	8	H1	Gouthwaite Clo.	6	D1	Harlow Rd.	17	D7	
Foxthorn Paddock	15	L6	Government Ho.	11	D4	Harold Ct.	11	C6	
Foxton	16	B8	Rd.			Harrison St.	14	J4	
Foxwood La.	16	A8	Gower Rd.	17	C8	Harrow Glade	7	E2	
Frances St.	19	G7	Granary Ct.	5	G5	Hartoft St.	19	G7	
Frederic St.	4	E5	Grange Cft.	19	G7	Haslemere Ct.	7	H1	
Freemans Ct.	12	E4	Grange Garth	19	G7	Hastings Clo.	7	E2	
Friargate	5	F6	Grange La.	16	A7	Hatfield Wk.	16	B8	
Friars Wk.	8	H3	Grange St.	19	G7	Haughton Rd.	7	F3	
Front St.	10	B6	Granger Av.	10	B6	Haverah Ct.	6	D2	
Fulford Cross	19	G8	Granger Pl.	10	B6	Hawkshead Clo.	16	A8	
Fulford Pk.	19	G9	Grantham Dr.	11	C6	Hawthorn Gro.	13	H4	
Fulford Rd.	19	G7	Grants Av.	19	H8	Hawthorn Spinney	8	H1	
Fulfordgate	19	H9	Granville Ter.	13	H6	Hawthorn St.	13	H4	
Furness Dr.	6	C1	Grape La.	4	F5	Hawthorn Ter.	8	G1	
			Grasmere Dr.	14	K5	Haxby Rd.	13	G4	
Gale Fm. Ct.	10	B6	Grasmere Gro.	6	D2	Haxby Rd., New	8	G2	
Gale La.	16	B7	Grassholme	16	B9	Earswick			
Galligap La.	15	L5	Gray St.	12	F6	Hazel Clo.	7	G1	
Gallops, The	16	A8	Grayshon Dr.	10	A4	Hazel Garth	9	K3	
Galmanhoe La.	12	F4	Green, The	10	B6	Hazelwood Av.	15	L6	
Galtres Av.	9	K3	Green Clo.	7	E2	Healey Gro.	8	H2	
Galtres Gro.	6	D3	Green Dykes La.	14	J6	Heath Clo.	17	D7	
Galtres Rd.	9	K3	Green La., Acomb	10	B6	Heath Cft.	19	H9	
Ganton Pl.	17	C9	Green La., Rawcliffe	6	D2	Heath Moor Dr.	19	H9	
Garburn Gro.	6	D2	Green Meadows	9	J3	Heather Bank	15	L6	
Garbutt Gro.	10	B5	Green Sward	9	J3	Heather Cft.	8	H1	
Garden Pl.	5	G5	Greencliffe Dr.	12	E4	Heathfield Rd.	14	J6	
Garden St.	13	G4	Greenfield Pk. Dr.	9	J3	Hebden Ri.	11	C6	

Name	Map	Grid
Helmsdale	16	B9
Hemlock Av.	8	H2
Hempland Av.	14	J4
Hempland Dr.	9	J3
Hempland La.	9	J3
Hendon Garth	7	E2
Herbert St.	13	H6
Herberts Way	9	J3
Herdsman Rd.	17	C9
Herman Wk.	16	B8
Hesketh Bank	15	L6
Heslington Ct.	20	K7
Heslington Cft.	19	H9
Heslington La.	19	H9
Heslington Rd.	13	H6
Hessay Pl.	10	A6
Hetherton St.	4	F5
Hewley Av.	14	J5
Heworth Grn.	13	G4
Heworth Hall Dr.	14	J4
Heworth Pl.	13	H4
Heworth Rd.	13	H4
Heworth Village	14	J4
High Fld.	15	L6
High Newbiggin St.	5	G4
High Oaks	9	K3
High Ousegate	4	F5
High Petergate	4	F5
Highcliffe Ct.	12	E4
Highmoor Clo.	17	C8
Highmoor Rd.	17	C8
Highthorn Rd.	8	H1
Hilbeck Gro.	14	K4
Hilda St.	13	H6
Hill St.	11	D6
Hill Vw.	9	K3
Hillcrest Gdns.	17	D8
Hillsborough Ter.	7	F3
Hinton Av.	16	B8
Hob Moor Dr.	17	D7
Hob Moor Ter.	17	D8
Hobgate	11	C6
Holgate Bri. Gdns.	12	E6
Holgate Lo. Dr.	11	C6
Holgate Rd.	11	D6
Hollands Rd.	19	H8
Holly Bank Gro.	17	D7
Holly Bank Rd.	17	D7
Holly Ter.	19	G7
Holmfield La.	20	J8
Holroyd Av.	14	J4
Holyrood Dr.	6	C1
Hope St.	5	G6
Horner St.	7	F3
Horseshoe, The	17	D9
Horsman Av.	13	G6
Hospital Flds.	19	G7
Hospital Flds. Rd.	19	G7
Hospital Flds. Ter.	19	G7
Hospital La.	12	F4
Hotham Av.	10	A6
Hothams Ct.	5	G6
Houndsway	16	A8
Howard Dr.	6	C1
Howard Link	6	C1
Howard St.	19	G7
Howe Hill Clo.	11	C5
Howe Hill Rd.	11	C5
Howe St.	11	C6
Hubert St.	18	E7
Huby Ct.	5	G6
Hudson Cres.	7	E3
Hudson St.	7	F3
Hull Rd.	14	J6
Hungate	5	G5
Hunt Ct.	5	G5
Hunters Way	17	D9
Huntington New La.	9	J1
Huntington Rd.	13	G4
Huntington Rd., New Earswick	8	H1
Huntsmans Wk.	16	A8
Hursts Yd.	5	G6
Hyrst Gro.	13	H4
Ilton Garth	7	E1
Ingleborough Av.	14	K5
Ingleton Wk.	14	J5
Ingram Av.	7	F2
Ings Vw.	6	C1
Ings Way	6	D3
Inman Ter.	11	C5
Intake Av.	7	F3
Invicta Ct.	16	B8
Irvine Way	16	A9
Irwin Av.	13	H4
Iver Clo.	10	B5
Ivy Pl.	8	G1
Jackson St.	13	G4
James Nicholson Link	6	D1
James St.	13	H6
Jamieson Ter.	18	E8
Jennifer Gro.	17	D7
Jervis Rd.	17	C8
Jewbury	5	G5
Jockey La.	9	J1
John St.	13	H4
Jorvik Clo.	10	B5
Jubbergate	4	F5
Jubilee Ter.	11	D4
Judges Ct.	4	F5
Julia Av.	9	K1
Juniper Clo.	8	G1
Jute Rd.	10	B5
Kathryn Av.	9	K1
Keats Clo.	6	D2
Kempton Clo.	17	C7
Kendrew Clo.	8	H1
Kenrick Pl.	10	B5
Kensal Ri.	19	G7
Kensington St.	18	F8
Kent St.	13	G6
Kentmere Dr.	6	D2
Kestrel Wd. Way	8	H1
Kettlestring La.	6	D1
Kettlestring La.	7	E1
Kexby Av.	13	H6
Kilburn Rd.	19	G7
Kimberlows Wds. Hill	15	L6
Kinbrace Dr.	16	A9
King St.	4	F6
Kings Acre	14	K4
Kings Ct.	5	G5
Kings Sq.	5	G5
Kings Staith	4	F6
Kingsland Ter.	11	D5
Kingsthorpe	11	C6
Kingsway N.	7	E3
Kingsway W.	17	C7
Kingswood Gro.	11	C6
Kir Cres.	10	B6
Kirk Vw.	10	B6
Kirkdale Rd.	15	L5
Kirkham Av.	8	G3
Kirkstone Dr.	14	J4
Kitchener St.	8	G3
Kitemere Pl.	16	A8
Knapton La.	10	A5
Knavesmire Cres.	18	E8
Knavesmire Rd.	18	E7
Knoll, The	16	A7
Kyme St.	4	F6
Laburnum Garth	9	J2
Lady Hamilton Gdns.	17	C7
Lady Hewley's Cotts.	5	G5
Lady Mill Garth	7	F3
Lady Peckitts Yd.	5	G5
Lady Rd.	7	F3
Lakeside Ct.	17	D8
Lambert Ct.	4	F6
Lamel St.	14	J6
Lancaster Way	7	E2
Landing La.	11	D4
Lang Av.	14	J5
Langdale Av.	14	K4
Langholme Dr.	10	B4
Langsett Gro.	6	D1
Lansdowne Ter.	13	H6
Lanshaw Cft.	6	D2
Larchfield	9	K3
Lastingham Ter.	19	G7
Lavender Gro.	11	C5
Lawnswood Dr.	6	D2
Lawnway	9	J3
Lawrence St.	13	H6
Lawson Rd.	17	D9
Layerthorpe	5	G5
Layerthorpe Bri.	5	G5
Lead Mill La.	5	G6
Leake St.	13	H6
Leeman Rd.	11	D5
Leeside	17	C8
Leicester Way	5	G6
Leighton Cft.	6	D2
Lendal	4	F5
Lendal Bri.	4	F5
Lerecroft Rd.	17	C8
Lesley Av.	19	H8
Leven Rd.	17	C9
Levisham St.	19	G7

Name	Page	Grid
Leyes, The	15	L6
Leyland Rd.	14	J4
Lichfield Ct.	18	E8
Lidgett Gro.	10	B4
Lilac Av.	14	K6
Lilling Av.	8	H2
Lime Av.	15	J4
Lime Tree Av.	8	G1
Lincoln St.	11	D4
Lindale	16	B9
Linden Gro.	7	E2
Lindley Rd.	6	D2
Lindley St.	11	D6
Lindley Wd. Gro.	6	D1
Lindsey Av.	11	C5
Link, The	19	H8
Link Av.	7	F2
Link Rd.	8	G1
Linton St.	11	C5
Lister Way	7	E3
Little Av.	7	F2
Little Hallfield Rd.	13	H5
Little Shambles	4	F5
Little Stonegate	4	F5
Livingstone St.	11	D5
Lloyd Clo.	20	K8
Lochrin Pl.	10	A5
Lockwood St.	13	G4
Long Clo. La.	5	G6
Longfield Ter.	4	E5
Longwood Link	6	D1
Longwood Rd.	6	D1
Lord Mayors Wk.	5	G4
Lorne St.	18	F8
Love La.	4	E6
Love La., Fulford	18	F8
Lovel Ho.	17	C8
Lovell St.	18	F7
Low La.	20	K8
Low Mill Clo.	15	L6
Low Moor Av.	19	H9
Low Ousegate	4	F5
Low Petergate	4	F5
Lower Darnborough St.	12	F6
Lower Ebor St.	12	F6
Lower Friargate	5	F6
Lower Priory St.	4	F6
Loweswater Rd.	6	C2
Lowfield La.	10	A5
Lowfields Dr.	10	B6
Lowick	16	B9
Lown Hill	16	B7
Lowther St.	13	G4
Lowther Ter.	4	E6
Loxley Clo.	6	D1
Lucas Av.	7	F3
Lumley Rd.	7	E3
Lycett Rd.	17	D9
Lydham Ct.	16	B8
Lyndale Av.	15	L6
Lynden Way	11	C6
Lysander Clo.	7	E1
Magnolia Gro.	7	G1
Maida Gro.	19	G7
Main Av.	13	H4
Main St.	20	K7
Main St., Fulford	13	G9
Malham Gro.	14	K5
Malt Shovel Ct.	5	G6
Malton Av.	13	H4
Malton Rd.	8	H3
Malton Way	6	D3
Malvern Av.	11	C5
Manor Dr. N.	11	C5
Manor Dr. S.	11	C5
Manor La.	6	C1
Manor Pk. Clo.	6	C1
Manor Pk. Gro.	6	C1
Manor Pk. Rd.	6	C1
Manor Way	6	C1
Mansfield St.	5	G5
Manthorpe Wk.	11	C5
Maple Ct.	8	G1
Maple Gro.	19	G8
Maplewood Paddock	16	B8
March St.	13	G4
Margaret Philipson Ct.	5	G5
Margaret St.	5	G6
Marjorie Waite Ct.	7	F3
Market St.	4	F5
Markham Cres.	13	G4
Markham St.	13	G4
Marlborough Clo.	6	C1
Marlborough Gro.	19	G7
Marston Av.	10	A6
Marston Cres.	10	A6
Martin Cheeseman Ct.	16	B8
Marygate	4	F5
Marygate La.	4	F5
Matmer Ct.	14	J6
Mattison Way	17	C7
Mayfield Gro.	17	D8
Maythorn Rd.	8	H1
Meadlands	14	K4
Meadow Ct.	17	D8
Meadow Way	9	J3
Meadowfields Dr.	8	G1
Melander Clo.	10	A5
Melbourne St.	13	G6
Melrose Clo.	14	J5
Melrose Ct.	14	J5
Melrosegate	14	J4
Melroses Yd.	5	G6
Melton Av.	6	D2
Melton Dr.	6	D2
Melwood Gro.	10	A4
Merchant Gate	5	G6
Merlin Covert	8	H1
Micklegate	4	F6
Micklegate Bar	4	F6
Middleham Av.	8	H2
Middlethorpe Dr.	17	D9
Middlethorpe Gro.	17	D9
Middleton Rd.	16	B7
Mildred Gro.	17	D7
Mill Gates	10	B4
Mill La.	13	H4
Mill Mt.	12	E6
Mill Mt. Ct.	12	E6
Mill St.	5	G6
Millfield Av.	14	J6
Millfield La.	14	J6
Millfield Rd.	18	F7
Milner St.	11	C6
Milson Gro.	14	J6
Milton Carr	6	D2
Milton St.	13	H6
Minster Av.	8	H1
Minster Gates	4	F5
Minster Yd.	4	F5
Mistral Ct.	8	G3
Mitchels La.	20	J8
Miterdale	16	B9
Moat Fld.	15	L5
Moatside Ct.	4	F5
Monk Av.	8	H3
Monk Bar Ct.	5	G5
Monkgate	5	G5
Monkgate Cloisters	5	G5
Monkton Rd.	8	H3
Montague St.	18	F8
Montrose Av.	8	G3
Moor Gro.	17	D8
Moor La., Acomb Park	16	A9
Moor La., Woodthorpe	17	C9
Moor Lea Av.	17	C8
Moorcroft Rd.	17	C9
Moore Av.	14	K5
Moorgarth Av.	17	D7
Moorgate	11	C6
Moorland Rd.	19	G8
Morrell Ct.	16	B8
Morritt Clo.	8	H2
Moss St.	4	E6
Mount, The	12	E6
Mount Ephraim	12	E6
Mount Par.	12	E6
Mount Vale	18	E7
Mount Vale Dr.	18	E7
Mowbray Dr.	10	B5
Muirfield Way	10	A5
Mulwith Clo.	14	J4
Muncastergate	8	H3
Murray St.	11	D6
Murrough Wilson Pl.	7	F3
Murton Way	15	M5
Museum St.	4	F5
Nairn Clo.	16	B9
Navigation Rd.	5	G5
Nelson St.	13	G4
Nelsons La.	17	D8
Nessgate	4	F5
Neville St.	13	G4
Neville Ter.	13	G4
Nevinson Gro.	19	H8
Nevis Way	16	A9
New La.	11	D6
New St.	4	F5

Rosslyn St.	12	E4	Sandcroft Rd.	17	C8	Sowerby Rd.	11	C5
Rougier St.	4	F5	Sandringham St.	19	G7	Spalding Av.	7	E3
Roundhill Link	6	D1	Sandstock Rd.	9	K3	Speculation St.	5	G6
Rowntree Av.	7	F3	Saville Gro.	7	E2	Spen La.	5	G5
Ruby St.	18	E7	Saxon Pl.	8	G3	Spencer St.	12	F6
Runswick Av.	10	A6	Scafell Clo.	6	C2	Spey Bank	16	B9
Russell St.	18	F7	Scaife Gdns.	8	G3	Spinney, The	17	D9
Russet Dr.	14	K5	Scaife Ms.	8	G3	Springfield Clo.	9	K3
Ryburn Clo.	6	D1	Scaife St.	8	G3	Springfield Ct.	11	D6
Rydal Av.	14	J4	Scarborough Ter.	12	F4	Springfield Way	9	K3
Ryecroft Av.	16	B9	Scarcroft Hill	18	E7	Spurr Ct.	16	B8
Ryecroft Clo.	9	K3	Scarcroft La.	4	F6	Spurriergate	4	F5
Rylatt Pl.	10	A6	Scarcroft Rd.	12	E6	Staindale Clo.	6	D1
			Scawton Av.	8	H1	Staithes Clo.	10	B6
Sadberge Ct.	14	K6	School La., Fulford	19	H9	Stamford St. E.	11	D5
Saddlebrook Ct.	16	B8	School La., Heslington	20	K7	Stamford St. W.	11	D5
St. Andrewgate	5	G5				Stanley St.	13	G4
St. Andrews Ct.	5	G5	School St.	11	C6	Starkey Cres.	14	J5
St. Anns Ct.	13	G6	Scott St.	18	F7	Station Av.	4	F5
St. Aubyns Pl.	18	E7	Scrope Av.	13	H5	Station Av., New Earswick	8	G1
St. Barnabas Ct.	11	D5	Seafire Clo.	7	E1	Station Ri.	4	F5
St. Benedict Rd.	12	F6	Seaton Clo. Av.	14	K5	Station Rd.	4	E5
St. Catherines Pl.	12	E6	Second Av.	13	H4	Sterne Av.	14	J5
St. Clements Gro.	18	F7	Sefton Av.	8	H2	Stirling Gro.	19	H8
St. Denys Rd.	5	G6	Segrave Wk.	11	C5	Stirrup Clo.	16	A8
St. Edwards Clo.	17	D8	Seldon Rd.	11	C5	Stockholm Clo.	19	G8
St. Georges Pl.	17	D7	Seventh Av.	13	H5	Stockton La.	9	J3
St. Helens Rd.	17	D8	Severus Av.	11	C5	Stonebow, The	5	G5
St. Helens Sq.	4	F5	Severus St.	11	C6	Stonegate	4	F5
St. James Ct.	12	E5	Seymour Gro.	13	H4	Stonegate Wk.	4	F5
St. James Mt.	18	E7	Shallowdale Gro.	15	L6	Stonelands Ct.	7	E2
St. James Pl.	17	C8	Shambles	5	G5	Stones Clo.	17	C7
St. Johns Cres.	13	G4	Shaws Ter.	4	E6	Stonethwaite	16	B9
St. Johns St.	5	G4	Shelley Gro.	6	D2	Stow Ct.	7	H1
St. Leonards Pl.	4	F5	Sherringham Dr.	16	B8	Strakers Pas.	5	G5
St. Lukes Gro.	7	F3	Sherwood Gro.	10	A4	Stratford Way	7	H1
St. Margarets Ter.	5	G6	Sherwood Gro., New Earswick	8	H1	Stray Garth	8	H3
St. Marks Gro.	6	C1	Shipton Rd.	6	D2	Stray Rd.	14	K4
St. Martins La.	4	F6	Shipton St.	7	F3	Straylands Gro.	9	J3
St. Marys	4	F5	Shirley Av.	10	B4	Stuart Rd.	17	C7
St. Marys Clo.	15	L6	Silver St.	4	F5	Stubden Gro.	6	D1
St. Marys La.	4	F5	Silverdale Ct.	16	B9	Sturdee Gro.	8	G3
St. Marys Sq.	5	G6	Sirocco Ct.	8	G3	Summerfield Rd.	16	B9
St. Marys Ter.	4	F5	Sitwell Gro.	10	B4	Surtees St.	7	F3
St. Maurices Rd.	5	G5	Siward St.	14	J6	Sussex Clo.	20	K7
St. Nicholas Pl.	13	H6	Sixth Av.	13	H5	Sussex Rd.	20	K7
St. Olaves Rd.	12	F4	Skeldergate	4	F6	Sutherland St.	18	E8
St. Oswalds Rd.	19	G8	Skeldergate Bri.	5	F6	Sutton Way	7	F2
St. Pauls Sq.	12	E6	Skelton Ct.	12	E4	Swale Av.	17	C8
St. Pauls Ter.	12	E6	Skewsby Gro.	8	H2	Swann St.	4	F6
St. Peters Gro.	12	E4	Skiddaw	16	B9	Swinegate	4	F5
St. Phillips Gro.	7	E3	Slessor Rd.	16	A8	Swinegate Ct.	5	F5
St. Sampsons Sq.	4	F5	Slingsby Gro.	17	D9	Swinerton Av.	11	D4
St. Saviourgate	5	G5	Smales St.	4	F6	Swinsty Ct.	6	D2
St. Saviours Pl.	5	G5	Smeaton Gro.	10	B5	Sycamore Pl.	4	E5
St. Stephens Rd.	16	B7	Smith Clo.	19	H8	Sycamore Ter.	4	E5
St. Stephens Sq.	16	B7	Somerset Rd.	8	G3	Sykes Clo.	12	F4
St. Swithins Wk.	11	C6	South Bank Av.	18	F7			
St. Thomas Pl.	13	G4	South Cotts.	6	C2	Tadcaster Rd.	17	D9
St. Thomas's Clo.	15	L5	South Esp.	5	F6	Tang Hall La.	14	J4
St. Wulstans Clo.	8	H3	South Par.	4	E6	Tanner Row	4	F5
Salisbury Rd.	11	D4	South Vw. Ter.	10	B6	Tanner St.	7	F3
Salisbury Ter.	11	D4	Southfield Cres.	17	C8	Tanners Moat	4	F5
Salmond Rd.	16	B8	Southlands Rd.	18	F7	Tarbert Cres.	16	A9
Sandacre Ct.	11	C4	Southolme Dr.	6	D2	Teck St.	12	F6
Sandcroft Clo.	17	C8						

Street	Map	Grid
Tedder Rd.	16	A7
Telford Ter.	18	E7
Temple Av.	14	K5
Templemead	8	H3
Ten Thorn La.	10	A5
Tennent Rd.	16	B7
Tennyson Av.	7	F3
Terry Av.	5	F6
Terry Av.	19	G7
Terry St.	18	F8
Thackerays Yd.	5	G6
Thanet Rd.	17	C8
Theresa Ct.	7	H2
Thief La.	13	H6
Third Av.	13	H4
Thirkleby Way	15	L5
Thirlmere Dr.	14	J4
Thomas St.	13	H6
Thoresby Rd.	16	A7
Thorn Nook	8	H3
Thornfield Av.	8	H2
Thornfield Dr.	8	H1
Thornton Moor Clo.	6	D1
Thornwood Covert	16	B8
Thorpe St.	18	F7
Tilmire Clo.	19	H8
Tisbury Rd.	11	D5
Tithe Clo.	16	A7
Toft Grn.	4	F6
Torridon Pl.	16	A9
Tostig Av.	10	B5
Tower Pl.	5	F6
Tower St.	13	G6
Townend St.	12	F4
Towton Av.	17	D7
Trafalgar St.	18	F7
Tranby Av.	15	L5
Trenchard Rd.	10	A4
Trenfield Ct.	11	D6
Trent Way	17	C9
Trentholme Dr.	18	E7
Trevor Gro.	11	D6
Trinity La.	4	F6
Troutbeck	16	B9
Troutsdale Av.	6	C1
Tudor Rd.	16	B7
Tuke Av.	14	K5
Turnberry Dr.	10	A5
Turners Cft.	20	J8
Turnmire Rd.	17	C8
Turpin Ct.	13	G6
Ullswater	16	B9
Union Ter.	12	F4
University Rd.	20	J7
Upper Hanover St.	11	D5
Upper Newborough St.	7	F3
Upper Price St.	12	F6
Upper St. Pauls Ter.	12	E6
Vanbrugh Dr.	15	L6
Vernon Rd.	6	C1
Vesper Dr.	10	B6
Vicarage Gdns.	14	K5
Victor St.	4	F6
Victoria Bar	4	F6
Victoria Ct.	11	D5
Victoria St.	12	F6
Viking Rd.	10	B5
Villa Gro.	13	H4
Village St.	10	A5
Vincent Way	16	B8
Vine St.	18	F7
Vyner St.	7	F3
Wains Gro.	17	C9
Wains Rd.	17	C8
Walker Dr.	16	B8
Walmgate	5	G6
Walmgate Bar	5	G6
Walney Rd.	14	J4
Walnut Clo.	20	J8
Walpole St.	8	G3
Walton Pl.	10	A6
Walworth St.	11	D4
Wandle, The	16	A7
Wansbeck	16	A9
Ward Ct.	12	F6
Warwick St.	13	G4
Wasdale Clo.	6	C2
Water End	11	C5
Water La.	7	E3
Watson St.	12	E6
Watson Ter.	12	E6
Waveney Gro.	7	F2
Waverley St.	13	G4
Waynefleet Gro.	14	J6
Weddall Clo.	17	D8
Welborn Clo.	14	J5
Welland Ri.	11	C5
Wellington Row	4	F5
Wellington St.	13	G6
Welton Av.	11	C4
Welwyn Dr.	19	H8
Wenlock Ter.	19	G7
Wensleydale Dr.	15	L5
Wentworth Rd.	18	E7
Werkdyke	5	G5
West Bank	11	C6
West Moor La.	20	J8
West Thorpe	17	C8
Westerdale Ct.	12	E4
Westfield Dr.	19	G8
Westfield Pl.	16	A7
Westholme Dr.	6	C2
Westlands Gro.	9	J3
Westminster Rd.	12	E4
Westwood Ter.	18	E8
Wetherby Rd.	10	A6
Wharfe Dr.	17	C8
Wharton Av.	7	E3
Wheatlands Gro.	10	B4
Whenby Gro.	8	H2
Whernside Av.	14	J4
Whin Clo.	17	D9
Whin Garth	17	D9
Whin Rd.	17	D9
Whip-Ma-Whop-Ma-Gate	5	G5
Whitby Av.	9	J3
Whitby Dr.	9	J3
White Cross Rd.	8	G3
White Ho. Dale	17	D7
White Ho. Dr.	17	D7
White Ho. Gdns.	17	D7
White Ho. Ri.	17	D7
White Rose Av.	8	G1
White Rose Gro.	8	G1
Whitestone Dr.	8	H1
Whitethorn Clo.	8	H1
Whitton Pl.	14	K6
Wigginton Rd.	7	F1
Wigginton Ter.	7	F3
Wilberforce Av.	7	F3
William Plows Av.	13	H6
Willis St.	13	G6
Willoughby Way	16	B8
Willow Bank	8	G1
Willow Glade	8	H1
Willow Gro.	9	J3
Wilsthorpe Gro.	19	H8
Wilton Ms.	11	D6
Wilton Ri.	11	D6
Winchester Av.	11	C5
Winchester Gro.	11	C5
Windermere	17	C9
Windmill La.	14	K6
Windmill Ri.	11	D6
Windsor Garth	17	C7
Windsor St.	18	E7
Winsear Gro.	6	D1
Winterscale Ct.	19	G7
Winterscale St.	19	G7
Wolfe Av.	14	J5
Wolsley St.	13	H6
Wolviston Av.	14	K6
Wood St.	13	H4
Woodford Pl.	17	C7
Woodhouse Gro.	14	J5
Woodlands Gro.	9	J3
Woodlea Av.	10	B5
Woodlea Bank	10	B5
Woodlea Cres.	10	B5
Woodlea Gro.	10	B5
Woodside Av.	14	J4
Woolnough Av.	14	K6
Worcester Dr.	14	K4
Wordsworth Cres.	16	B9
Wrays Av.	8	H2
Wrays Cotts.	8	H2
Wycliffe Av.	14	K6
Wydale Rd.	15	L5
Yarburgh Gro.	11	C5
Yarburgh Way	15	L6
Yearsley Cres.	8	G3
Yearsley Gro.	8	H2
Yew Tree Ms.	15	L5
York Rd.	10	B6